How to be an Alien

GEORGE MIKES

Nicolas Bentley
drew the pictures

Level 3

Retold by Karen Holmes
Series Editors: Andy Hopkins and Jocelyn Potter

Pearson Education Limited
Edinburgh Gate, Harlow,
Essex CM20 2JE, England
and Associated Companies throughout the world.

ISBN 0 582 468272

First published by André Deutsch 1946
Copyright 1946 by George Mikes and Nicolas Bentley
This adaptation first published by Penguin Books 1998
Published by Addison Wesley Longman Limited and Penguin Books Ltd. 1998
This edition first published 2000

Text copyright © Karen Holmes 1998
All illustrations copyright © Nicolas Bentley 1946
All rights reserved

Typeset by Digital Type, London
Set in 11/14pt Bembo
Printed in Spain by Mateu Cromo, S. A. Pinto (Madrid)

Published by Pearson Education Limited in association with
Penguin Books Ltd, both companies being subsidiaries of Pearson Plc

For a complete list of the titles available in the Penguin Readers series please write to your local
Pearson Education office or to: Marketing Department, Penguin Longman Publishing,
5 Bentinck Street, London W1M 5RN.

Contents

Introduction

The weather is the most important subject in the land. In Europe, people say, 'He is the type of person who talks about the weather,' to show that somebody is very boring. In England, the weather is always an interesting, exciting subject and you must be good at talking about it.

George Mikes wrote this book to tell the English what he thought about them. He is both funny and rude about the strange things English people do and say – the things that make them different from other Europeans. In this book you will learn many useful rules about being English. You will learn how to talk about the weather, and what to say when somebody brings you a cup of tea at 5 o'clock in the morning. You will discover what the English *really* think of clever people and doctors. This book will help you to be more like the English. As George Mikes says: 'If you are like the English, they think you are funny. If you are not like them, they think you are even funnier.'

George Mikes was born in Hungary in 1921. He studied law at Budapest University, and then began to write for newspapers. He came to London for two weeks just before the Second World War began, and made England his home for the rest of his life. During the war he worked for the BBC, making radio programmes for Hungary.

He wrote *How to be an Alien* in 1946. He did not want to write an amusing book, but thousands of English people bought it and found it very funny. He wrote many other books about foreigners and English people. The story of his life, *How to be Seventy*, went on sale in bookshops on his seventieth birthday in 1982. He died in 1987.

I wrote this book in 1946. Many people bought it and said kind things about it. I was surprised and pleased but I was also unhappy that they liked it.

I will explain.

It is very nice when a lot of people buy a book by a new writer. I'm sorry, 'very nice' is not an English thing to say. It is *not unpleasant* when a lot of readers like a new book.

Why was I unhappy? I wrote this book to tell the English what I thought about them, or 'where to get off' as they say. I thought I was brave. I thought, 'This book is going to make the English angry!' But no storm came! The English only said that my book was 'quite amusing'. I was very unhappy.

Then, a few weeks later, I heard about a woman who gave this book to her husband because she thought it was 'quite amusing'. The man sat down, put his feet up, and read the book. His face became darker and darker. When he finished the book, he stood up and said, 'Rude! Very, very rude!' He threw the book into the fire.

What a good Englishman! He said just the right thing, and I felt much better. I hoped to meet more men like him, but I never found another Englishman who did not like the book.

I have written many more books since then but nobody remembers them. Everybody thinks *How to be an Alien* is the only book that I have ever written. This is a problem. I am now in the middle of writing a very large and serious book, 750 pages long, about old Sumeria. I will win the Nobel Prize for it. It will make no difference; people will still think *How to be an Alien* is the only book that I have ever written.

People ask me, 'When are you going to write another *How to be an Alien*?' I am sure they mean to be kind, but they cannot quite understand my quiet reply: 'Never, I hope.'

I think I am the right person to write about 'how to be an alien'. I *am* an alien. I have been an alien all my life. I first understood that I was an alien when I was twenty-six years old. In my country, Hungary, everybody was an alien so I did not think I was very different or unusual. Then I came to England and learned that I was different. This was an unpleasant surprise.

I learned immediately that I was an alien. People learn all important things in a few seconds. A long time ago I spent a lot of time with a young woman who was very proud of being English. One day, to my great surprise, she asked me to marry her.

'No,' I replied, 'I cannot marry you. My mother does not want me to marry a foreigner.'

She looked surprised and replied, 'Me, a foreigner? What a funny thing to say. I'm English. *You* are the foreigner! And your mother is a foreigner, too!'

I did not agree. 'Am I a foreigner in Budapest, too?' I asked.

'Everywhere,' she said. 'If it's true that you're an alien in England, it's also true in Hungary and North Borneo and Venezuela and everywhere.'

She was right, of course, and I was quite unhappy about it. There is no way out of it. Other people can change. A criminal can perhaps change his ways and become a better person but a foreigner cannot change. A foreigner is always a foreigner. He can become British, perhaps; he can never become truly *English*.

So it is better to understand that you are always a foreigner. Maybe some English people will forgive you. They will be polite to you. They will ask you into their homes and they will be kind to you. The English keep dogs and cats and they are happy to keep a few foreigners, too. This book offers you some rules about being an alien in England. Study them carefully. They will help you to be more like the English. If you are like the English, they think you are funny. If you are not like them, they think you are even funnier.

G.M.

Chapter 1   A Warning to Beginners

In England everything is different. You must understand that when people say 'England', they sometimes mean 'Great Britain' (England, Scotland and Wales), sometimes 'the United Kingdom' (England, Scotland, Wales and Northern Ireland), sometimes the 'British Isles' (England, Scotland, Wales, Northern Ireland and the Republic of Ireland) – but never just England.

On Sundays in Europe, the poorest person wears his best clothes and the life of the country becomes happy, bright and colourful; on Sundays in England, the richest people wear their oldest clothes and the country becomes dark and sad. In Europe nobody talks about the weather; in England, you have to say 'Nice day, isn't it?' about two hundred times every day, or people think you are a bit boring. In Europe you get Sunday newspapers on Monday. In England, a strange country, you get Sunday newspapers on Sunday.

On a European bus the driver uses the bell if he wants to drive on past a bus-stop without stopping. In England you use the bell when you want the bus to stop. In Europe people like their cats but in England they love their cats more than their family. In Europe, people eat good food. In England people think that good manners at the table are more important than the food you get to eat. The English eat bad food but they say it tastes good.

In Europe important people speak loudly and clearly; in England they learn to speak slowly and quietly so you cannot understand them. In Europe, clever people show that they are clever by talking about Aristotle, Horace and Montaigne; in England only stupid people try to show how clever they are. The

*On Sundays in England, the richest people wear their oldest clothes
and the country becomes sad and dark.*

only people who talk about Latin and Greek writers are those who have not read them.

In Europe, almost every country, big or small, fights wars to show they are the best; the English fight wars against those people who think they are the best. The English already know which country is *really* the best. Europeans cry and quickly get angry; instead of this the English just laugh quietly at their problems. In Europe people are either honest with you or they lie to you; in England people almost never lie, but they are almost never quite honest with you either. Many Europeans think that life is a game; the English think cricket is a game.

Chapter 2   Introducing People

This part of the book tells you how to introduce people to other people.

Most importantly, when you introduce strangers, do not say their name so that the other person is able to hear it. Usually this is not a problem because nobody can understand your accent.

If somebody introduces you to a stranger, there are two important rules to follow.

1 If he puts out his hand to shake yours, do not take it. Smile and wait. When he stops trying to shake your hand, try to shake *his*. Repeat this game all afternoon or evening. Quite possibly this will be the most amusing part of your afternoon or evening.

2 The introductions are finished and your new friend asks if you are well: 'How do you do? ' But do not forget: he does not really want to know. To him it does not matter if you are well or if you are dying of a terrible illness. Do not answer. Your conversation will be like this:

HE: 'How do you do?'

If he puts out his hand to shake yours, do not take it. When he stops trying to shake your hand, try to shake his.

YOU:'Quite good health. Not sleeping very well. Left foot hurts a bit. One or two stomach problems.'

A conversation like this is un-English, and unforgivable. When you meet somebody, never say, 'Pleased to meet you.' English people think this is very rude.

And one other thing: do not call foreign lawyers, teachers, doctors, dentists or shopkeepers 'Doctor'. Everybody knows that the little word 'doctor' means that you are a central European. It is not a good thing to be a central European in England, so you do not want people to remember.

Chapter 3   The Weather

This is the most important subject in the land. In Europe, people say, 'He is the type of person who talks about the weather,' to show that somebody is very boring. In England, the weather is always an interesting, exciting subject and you must be good at talking about it.

Chapter 4   Examples for Conversation

For Good Weather

'Nice day, isn't it?'
'Isn't it *beauti*ful?'
'The sun ...'
'Isn't it wonderful?'
'Yes, wonderful, isn't it?'
'It's so nice and hot ...'
'I think it's so nice when it's hot, isn't it?'
'I really love it, don't you?'

'Terrible day, isn't it?'

'Isn't it unpleasant?'

'The rain . . . I don't like the rain.'

'Just think — a day like this in July. It rains in the morning, then a bit of sun and then rain, rain, rain, all day.'

'I remember the same July day in 1936 . . .'

'Yes, I remember too.'

'Or was it 1928?'

'Yes, it was.'

'Or in 1939?'

'Yes, that's right.'

Now look at the last few sentences of this conversation. You can see a very important rule: you must always agree with other people when you talk about the weather. If it is raining and snowing and the wind is knocking down trees, and someone says, 'Nice day, isn't it?' answer immediately, 'Isn't it wonderful?'

Learn these conversations by heart. You can use them again and again. If you repeat these conversations every day for the rest of your life, it is possible that people will think you are clever, polite and amusing.

Listen to the weather reports on the radio and you will hear different weather reports for different people. There is always a different report for farmers. For example, you hear, 'Tomorrow it will be cloudy and cold. There will be a lot of rain.'

Then, immediately after this you hear, 'Weather report for farmers. It will be bright and warm and there will be a lot of sunshine.'

Farmers do important work for the country, so they need better weather, you see.

Often the radio tells you that it is a nice day but then you look

If it is raining and someone says, 'Nice day, isn't it?'
answer immediately, 'Isn't it wonderful?'

outside and see that it is raining or snowing. Sometimes the radio says it is a rainy day and you see that the sun is shining brightly. This is not because the weather people have made a mistake. It is because they have reported the *right* weather as they want it to be but then some troublesome weather from another part of the world moves in across Britain and changes the weather picture. If British weather has to mix with foreign weather, things are not looking very good.

Chapter 5   Soul: Not Quite Saying What You Mean

Foreigners have souls; the English do not have souls. In Europe you find many people who look sad. This is soul. The worst kind of soul belongs to the Slav people. Slavs are usually very deep thinkers. They say things like this: 'Sometimes I am so happy and sometimes I am so sad. Can you explain why?' (You cannot explain, do not try.) Or perhaps they say, 'I want to be in some other place, not here.' (Do not say, 'I'd like you to be in some other place, too.')

All this is very deep. It is soul, just soul. But the English have no soul. Instead they say less than they mean. For example, if a European boy wants to tell a girl that he loves her, he goes down on his knees and tells her she is the sweetest, most beautiful and wonderful person in the world. She has something in her, something special, and he cannot live one more minute without her.

In Europe you find many people who look sad. This is soul.

Sometimes, to make all this quite clear, he shoots himself. This happens every day in European countries where people have soul.

In England the boy puts his hand on the girl's shoulder and says quietly, 'You're all right, you know.'

If he really loves her, he says, 'I really quite like you, in fact.'

If he wants to marry a girl, he says, 'I say ... would you ...?'

If he wants to sleep with her, 'I say ... shall we ...?'

Chapter 6   Tea

Tea was once a good drink; with lemon and sugar it tastes very pleasant. But then the British decided to put cold milk and no sugar into it. They made it colourless and tasteless. In the hands of the English, tea became an unpleasant drink, like dirty water, but they still call it 'tea'.

Tea is the most important drink in Great Britain and Ireland. You must never say, 'I do not want a cup of tea,' or people will think that you are very strange and very foreign.

In an English home, you get a cup of tea at five o'clock in the morning when you are still trying to sleep. If your friend brings you a cup of tea and you wake from your sweetest morning sleep, you must not say, 'I think you are most unkind to wake me up and I'd like to shoot you!' You must smile your best five o'clock smile and say, 'Thank you so much. I do love a cup of tea at this time of the morning.' When your friend leaves the room, you can throw the tea down the toilet.

Then you have tea for breakfast; you have tea at eleven o'clock in the morning; then after lunch; then you have tea at 'tea-time' (about four o'clock in the afternoon); then after supper; and again at eleven o'clock at night.

You must drink more cups of tea if the weather is hot; if it is cold; if you are tired; if anybody thinks you are tired; if you are afraid; before you go out; if you are out; if you have just returned home; if you want a cup; if you do not want a cup; if you have not had a cup for some time; if you have just had a cup.

You must not follow my example. I sleep at five o'clock in the morning; I have coffee for breakfast; I drink black coffee again and again during the day; I drink strange and unusual teas (with no milk) at tea-time.

I have these funny foreign ways . . . and my poor wife (who was once a good Englishwoman) now has them too, I'm sorry to say.

Chapter 7   Sex

European men and women have sex lives; English men and women have hot-water bottles.

Chapter 8   The Language

When I arrived in England I thought that I knew English. After I'd been here an hour I realized I did not understand one word. In my first week I learned a little of the language, but after seven years I knew that I could never use it really well. This is sad, but nobody speaks English perfectly.

Remember that those five hundred words the ordinary Englishman uses most are not all the words in the language. You can learn another five hundred and another five thousand and another fifty thousand words after that and you will still find another fifty thousand you have never heard of. Nobody has heard of them.

If you live in England for a long time you will be very surprised to find that the word nice is not the only adjective in the English language. For the first three years you do not need to learn or use any other adjectives. You can say that the weather is nice, a restaurant is nice, Mr So-and-so is nice, Mrs So-and-so's clothes are nice, you had a nice time, and all this will be very nice.

You must decide about your accent. You will have your foreign accent all right but many people like to mix it with another accent. I knew a Polish Jew who had a strong Yiddish-Irish accent. People thought he was very interesting.

The easiest way to show that you have a good accent (or no foreign accent) is to hold a pipe or cigar in your mouth, to speak through your teeth and finish all your sentences with the question: 'isn't it?' People will not understand you, but they will think that you probably speak very good English.

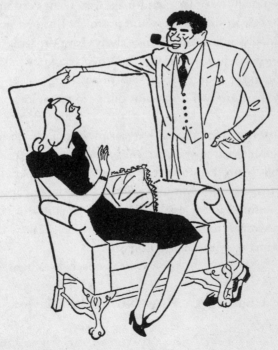

Hold a pipe in your mouth, speak through your teeth and finish all your sentences with the question: 'isn't it?'

Many foreigners try hard to speak with an Oxford accent. The city of Oxford has a famous university. If you have an Oxford accent, people think that you mix with clever people and that you are very intelligent. But the Oxford accent hurts your throat and is hard to use all the time.

Sometimes you can forget to use it, speak with your foreign accent and then where are you? People will laugh at you. The best way to look clever is to use long words, of course. These words are often old Latin and Greek words, which the English language has taken in. Many foreigners have learned Latin and Greek in school and they find that (a) it is much easier to learn these words than the much shorter English words; (b) these words are usually very long and make you seem very intelligent when you talk to shopkeepers and postmen. But be careful with all these long words – they do not always have the same meaning as they once had in Latin or Greek. When you know all the long words, remember to learn some short ones, too.

Finally there are two important things to remember:

1 Do not forget that it is much easier to write in English than to speak English, because you can *write* without a foreign accent.
2 On a bus or in the street it is better to speak quietly in good German than to shout loudly in bad English. Anyway, all this language business is not easy. After eight years in this country, a very kind woman told me the other day, 'You speak with a very good accent, but without any English.'

Chapter 9 How Not to Be Clever

'You foreigners are so clever,' a woman said to me some years ago. I know many foreigners who are stupid. I thought she was being kind but not quite honest.

Now I know that she was *not* being kind. These words showed that she did not like foreigners. Look at the word 'clever' in any English dictionary. These dictionaries say 'clever' means, 'quick, intelligent'. These are nice adjectives but the dictionaries are all a little out of date. A modern Englishman uses the word 'clever' to mean 'possibly a bit dishonest, un-English, un-Scottish, un-Welsh'.

In England it is bad manners to be clever or proud of your intelligence. Perhaps you *know* that two and two make four, but you must never *say* that two and two make four.

The Englishman is shy and quiet. He does not show that he is clever. He uses few words but he says a lot with them. A European, for example, looks at a beautiful place and says, 'This place looks like Utrecht, where a war ended on the 11th April, 1713. The river over there is like the Guadalquivir in the Sierra de Cazorla and is 650 kilometres long. It runs south-west to the Atlantic Ocean. Rivers . . . what does So-and-so say? . . . did I tell you about . . .?'

You cannot speak like this in England. An Englishman looks at the same place. He is silent for two or three hours and then he says, 'It's pretty, isn't it?'

An English girl, of course, understands it is not clever to know if Budapest is the capital city of Romania, Hungary or Bulgaria. It is so much nicer to ask, when someone speaks of Barbados, Banska Bystrica or Fiji, 'Oh, those little islands . . . are they British?' (Once, they usually were.)

Chapter 10   How to Be Rude

It is easy to be rude in Europe. You just shout and call people animal names. To be very rude, you can make up terrible stories about them.

In England people are rude in a very different way. If somebody tells you an untrue story, in Europe you say, 'You are a

It is easy to be rude in Europe. You just shout and call people animal names.

liar, sir.' In England you just say, 'Oh, is that so?' Or, 'That's quite an unusual story, isn't it?'

A few years ago, when I knew only about ten words of English and used them all wrong, I went for a job. The man who saw me said quietly, 'I'm afraid your English is a bit unusual.' In any European language, this means, 'Kick this man out of the office!'

A hundred years ago, if somebody made the Sultan of Turkey or the Czar of Russia angry, they cut off the person's head immediately. But when somebody made the English queen angry, she said, 'We are not amused,' and the English are still, to this day, very proud of their queen for being so rude.

Terribly rude things to say are: 'I'm afraid that ...', 'How strange that ...' and 'I'm sorry, but ...' You must look very serious when you say these things.

It is true that sometimes you hear people shout, 'Get out of here!' or 'Shut your big mouth!' or 'Dirty pig!' etc. This is very un-English. Foreigners who lived in England hundreds of years ago probably introduced these things to the English language.

Chapter 11   How to Compromise

For the British, compromise is very important. Compromise means that you bring together everything that is bad. For example, English people agree to go to a party but then do not speak to anyone.

In an English house you can see that the English compromise. It is all right for their houses to have walls and a roof, but they must be as cold inside as the garden outside. It is all right to have a fire in an English home, but if you sit in front of it, your face is hot but your back is cold. It is a compromise; it answers the problem of how to burn and catch a cold at the same time.

In an English pub, you can have a drink at five minutes *after* six but you cannot have a drink at five minutes *before* six. This is a compromise. To drink too much between three o'clock and six o'clock in the afternoon, you must stay at home.

The English language is a compromise between sensible, easy words and words which nobody understands.

A visit to the cinema is a compromise: you must queue uncomfortably for three hours to get inside the cinema so that you can be comfortable for one hour during the film.

English weather is a compromise between rain and snow. In fact, almost everything about life in England is a compromise.

Chapter 12   How to Be a Hypocrite

If you want to be really and truly British, you must become a hypocrite.

Now, how do you become a hypocrite?

As some people say an example explains things best, I'll try this way.

I was having a drink with an English friend in a pub. We were sitting on high chairs near the bar when suddenly there was a fight and some shooting in the street. I was truly and honestly frightened. A few seconds later I looked for my friend but I couldn't see him anywhere. At last I saw that he was lying on the floor. When he realized we were safe in the pub, he stood up. He turned to me and smiled. 'Good God!' he said. 'You were frightened! You didn't even move!'

Chapter 13   Small Pleasures

It is important to learn to enjoy small pleasures because that is terribly English. All serious Englishmen play cricket and other games. During the war, the French thought the English were childish because they played football and children's games when they were not fighting.

Boring and important foreigners cannot understand these small pleasures. They ask: why do important men in the British government stand up and sing children's songs? Why do serious businessmen play with children's trains while their children sit in the next room learning their lessons? Why, more than anything else, do grown-up people want to hit a little ball into a small hole? (This is a *very* popular sport in England.) Why are the great men in government who saved England in the war only called 'quite good men'? Foreigners want to know: why do English people sing when nobody is in the room? If somebody *is* in the room, the English will stay silent for months.

Chapter 14 Favourite Things

In England, people do not often get excited. They do not enjoy many things but they love to queue.

In Europe, if people are waiting at a bus-stop they look bored and half asleep. When the bus arrives they fight to get on it. Most of them leave on the bus and some are very lucky and leave in an ambulance. One Englishman waits at a bus-stop and, even if there are no other people there, he starts a queue.

The biggest and best queues are in front of cinemas. These queues have large cards that say: Queue here for 4s 6d; Queue here for 9s 3d; Queue here for 16s 8d. Nobody goes to a cinema if it does not have cards telling customers to queue.

At weekends, an Englishman queues up at the bus-stop, travels out to Richmond, queues up for a boat, then queues up for tea, then queues up for ice cream, then queues up some more because it is fun, then queues up at the bus-stop when he wants to go home. He has a very good time.

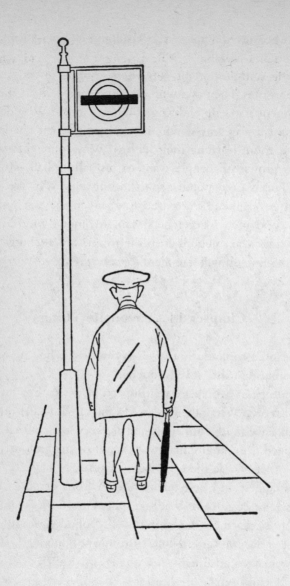

One Englishman waits at a bus-stop and, even if there are no other people there, he starts a queue.

Many English families spend pleasant evenings at home just by queuing for a few hours. The parents are very sad when the children leave them and queue up to go to bed.

Chapter 15   Remember

If you go for a walk with a friend in England, don't say a single word for hours; if you go for a walk with your dog, talk to it all the time.

PART 2   LESS IMPORTANT RULES AND SOME SPECIAL EXAMPLES

Chapter 16   A Bloomsbury Intellectual★

Bloomsbury intellectuals do not want to look like each other so they all wear the same clothes: brown trousers, yellow shirt, green and blue jacket. They also like purple shoes.

They choose these clothes very carefully to show that they do not think clothes are important.

It is terribly important that the B.I. always has a three-day beard because shaving is only for ordinary people. (Some B.I.s think washing is only for ordinary people, too.) At first it is quite difficult to shave a four-day beard so that it looks like a three-day beard but, with practice, a B.I. can always have a perfect three-day beard.

To be a Bloomsbury Intellectual you must be rude, because you have to show day and night that the silly little rules of the country are not meant for *you*. If you find it is too difficult to stop being polite, to stop saying 'Hello', and 'How do you do?'

★ Bloomsbury is a part of Central London, near London University. An intellectual is somebody who *thinks* he is very clever.

and 'Thank you' etc., then go to a Bloomsbury school for bad manners. There you can learn to be rude. After two weeks, you will not feel bad if, on purpose, you stand on the foot of somebody you do not like as you get on the bus.

Finally, remember the most important rule. Always be different! Only think and talk about new ideas. This is not difficult; just think and talk about the same new ideas that other Bloomsbury Intellectuals think and talk about.

Chapter 17   Mayfair Playboy*

Put the little word *de* in front of your name. This makes people think that you are important. I knew a man called Leo Rosenberg from Graz who called himself Lionel de Rosenberg and everyone thought he was an Austrian prince. Understand that the most important thing in life is to have a nice time, go to nice places and meet nice people. (Now: to have a nice time you must drink too much; nice places are great hotels and large houses with a lot of music and no books; nice people say stupid things in good English – unpleasant people say clever things with a bad accent.) In the old days the man who had no money was not a gentleman. Today, in Mayfair, things are different. A gentleman can have money or borrow money from his friends; the important thing is that even if he is very poor he must not do useful work.

Always laugh if someone says something amusing. Be polite, but do not be serious. Laugh at everything that you are not intelligent enough to understand. Don't forget that your clothes – your trousers, ties and shirts – are the most important things in your life. Always be drunk after 6.30 p.m.

* Mayfair is part of London where very rich people live. A playboy is a man – usually young and unmarried – who enjoys life all the time.

Chapter 18   How to Be A Film-Maker

To become a really great British film-maker, you need to have a little foreign blood in you.

The first thing a British film-maker wants to do is to teach Hollywood how to make good films. To do this you must not try to make films about American subjects. Here is the subject for an American film. Do not use it.

A young man from Carthage (Kentucky), who can sing beautifully, goes to town. After many difficulties he becomes New York's most famous singer. At the same time he falls in love with a poor girl who works in a local shop. She is very beautiful but nobody knows that she also has the best voice in the city. She helps her lover when she sings a song in his theatre in front of six million people. The young and very famous singer marries the girl.

Here is an example of a serious and 'deep' American film: a happy but very poor young man in New Golders Green (Alabama) becomes very rich selling thousands of machines to other poor people. The richer he becomes, the more unhappy he is – everybody knows that money cannot make you happy; it is better to be poor and have no job. The young man buys seven big cars and three aeroplanes and becomes more unhappy. He builds a large and beautiful house and is very, very unhappy. When the woman he has loved for fifteen years finally says she will marry him, he cries for three days.

This story is very deep; it has soul. To show the film has soul, the cameraman takes interesting and surprising pictures of the filmstars. He takes photographs of the bottom of their feet and the tops of their heads. Everybody is happy with this new way of making films and thinks that the film-maker is very clever.

English film-makers are different. They know that not all the people who watch films are stupid and some of them can enjoy intelligent films.

Here are some important rules you must remember if you want to make a really and truly British film:

1 The famous writer, Mr Noel Coward, says that he met a man who once saw a Cockney. Cockneys are people who were born in the east of London. They cannot speak good English and they cannot say the letter 'h', but they are kind and have big hearts. Now all good people in films are Cockneys and every British film must have a Cockney.

2 Nothing is too good for a British film-maker – he must have the best. I have heard of a man (I do not know if this story is true, but it shows how British film-makers work) who made a film about Egypt. He built a sphinx in England. He sailed to Egypt (where there is a real sphinx) and he took his own sphinx. He was quite right to do this, because the Egyptian sphinx is very old and great film-makers do not use anything old. Secondly, the old sphinx is good enough for the Egyptians but the Egyptians are foreigners; British film-makers need something better.

3 To make a good film, change the story and the people a little. Make *Peter Pan* (a famous children's story) into a murder story. Make the *Concise Oxford Dictionary* into a funny film and sing all the words!

Chapter 19   Driving Cars

It is the same to drive a car in England as any other country. To change a car wheel in the wind and rain is as pleasant outside London as outside Rio de Janeiro. It is no more funny to try to start your car in Moscow than in Manchester. If your car stops moving anywhere – in Sydney or in Edinburgh – you will still have to push it.

But the English car driver is different from the European car

The famous writer, Mr Noel Coward, says that he met a man who once saw a Cockney.

driver so there are some things you must remember when you drive in England.

1 In English towns you must drive at thirty miles an hour. The police watch carefully for drivers who go too fast. The fight against bad drivers is very clever and very English. It is difficult to know if a police car is following you but if you are very intelligent and have very good eyes, you will see these cars. Remember:
(a) the police always drive blue cars
(b) three policemen sit in each car

It is no more funny to try to start your car in Moscow than in Manchester.

(c) you can read the word POLICE in large letters on the front and back of these cars.

2 I think England is the only country in the world where you must leave your car lights on when you park your car at night in a busy street with lots of street lights. Then, when you come back to the car, you cannot start it again. The car will not work; it is dead. But this is wonderful! There are fewer cars on the road and the number of road crashes goes down. This makes the roads safe!

3 Only car drivers know the answer to this difficult question: What are taxis for? A person who is walking and looking for a taxi knows they are not there to carry passengers.

Taxis are on the road to teach good manners to car drivers. They teach us never to be too brave; they make us remember that we do not know what the next minute will bring for us, if we can drive down the road or if a taxi will hit us from the back or the side . . .

4 Car drivers are at war with other people.

If you park your car in the City, the West End of London or many other places, two or three policemen will run up and tell you, 'You cannot park here! Move along!' So where can you park? The policemen do not know. 'Try a place thirty miles down the road near the sea in the village of Minchinhampton,' they say. ' Three cars can park there for half an hour on Sunday morning between 7 and 8 a.m.'

The police are right. Cars need to move, and move fast, not stop.

Some people think that the police are wrong. They do not want to drive their cars, they think cars are built to park and not to move. These people drive out of Central London to the great park Hampstead Heath or to the river at Richmond on a beautiful sunny day. They park their cars, close the windows and go to sleep. They are very uncomfortable and they sleep badly, of course – it is hot. But they say they are 'having a nice afternoon's holiday'.

Chapter 20   Three Games for Bus Drivers

If you become a bus driver in England, play these three very amusing games.

1 Drive along the street and suddenly turn right. Don't tell anybody. It is very amusing. Other drivers do not know that you are going to turn right and they crash into your big bus with their little cars.

2 Drive up to a bus-stop. Hide behind a large lorry or another bus. Then, when you get to the bus-stop, do not stop but drive away fast. It is very amusing to see the faces of the people who

It is very amusing to see the faces of the people who
wanted to get on your bus.

wanted to get on your bus. They are angry – they will have to wait all day for another bus.

3 If you stop the bus at a bus-stop, drive away again quickly and suddenly. If you are lucky, people will try to get on your bus and they will fall off when you drive away. It is very amusing for the driver to see these people fall off the bus. (Sometimes people fall down and get dirty or sometimes they break their leg. And they always get angry. Some people are very boring. They won't laugh at anything.)

Chapter 21   How to Plan a Town

The English like to be uncomfortable. They think that this makes them strong. Only weak people from Europe live in comfortable, pleasant towns.

People who build English towns want to make everything difficult. In Europe, doctors, lawyers and people who sell books have their houses and shops together in different parts of the town so you can always find a good (or a bad but expensive) doctor anywhere. In England, your address is important. In London, all the doctors live and work in Harley Street, all the lawyers are in Lincoln's Inn Fields and all the book-sellers are in the Charing Cross Road. The newspaper offices are all in Fleet Street, the people who make men's clothes are all in Saville Row and the car salesmen are in Great Portland Street. Theatres are near Piccadilly Circus and cinemas are in Leicester Square. Soon all the fruit and vegetable shops will move to Hornsey Lane, all the butchers to the Mile End Road and all the men's toilets to Bloomsbury.

Now, I want to tell you about how to build an English town. You must understand that an English town is built to make life as difficult as possible for foreigners.

1 First of all, never build a straight street. The English do not like to be able to see two ends of a street. Make bends in the streets or make them S-shaped. The letters L, T, V, Y, W, and O also make good shapes for streets. It would please the Greeks if you built a few ø or ß-shaped streets. Maybe you could build streets like Russian or Chinese letters, too.

2 Never build all the houses in a street in a straight line. The British are free people so they are free to build their houses in circles.

3 Make sure that nobody can find the houses. European people put the numbers 1, 3, 5, 7 on one side of the street and 2, 4, 6, 8 on the other side of the street. The small numbers always start from the north or west. In England they start the numbers at one end of the street, then suddenly stop and continue the numbers on the opposite side going back the other way.

You can leave out some numbers and you can continue the numbers in a side street; you can also give the same number to two or three houses.

And you can do more! Many people do not have numbers on their houses; instead they give their houses names. It is very amusing to go to a street with three hundred and fifty houses and to look for a house called 'The House'. Or you can visit a house called 'Orange Tree House' and find that there are three apple trees in the garden.

4 If the road bends, give a different name to the second part of it but, if it bends a lot so it is really two different streets, you can keep the same name. If the street is long and straight, give it many different names (High Holborn, New Oxford Street, Oxford Street, Bayswater Road, Notting Hill Gate, Holland Park, etc.★)

5 Some clever foreigners will find the street that they want, so

★ These are all parts of one very long, straight street in the centre of London.

make it harder for them. Call the street by another name. Don't just call it a 'street', call it a 'road', 'way', 'park', 'garden', etc.

Now try this:

(a) Put all the streets with the same name in the same part of town: Belsize Park, Belsize Street, Belsize Gardens, Belsize Way, etc.

(b) Put a number of streets with the same name in *different* parts of the town. If you have twenty Princes Squares and twenty Warwick Roads, nobody will be able to find the right place.

6 Paint the street name in large letters on a piece of wood. Hide this piece of wood carefully. Put it very high on the wall or very low behind the flowers in someone's garden, or in a shadow – anywhere where people cannot see it. Even better, take the street name to your bank and ask the bank to keep it for you. If you don't, somebody will find out where they are.

7 To really worry foreigners, make four streets into squares like this (see the picture below). In this way it is possible to build a street which has two different names – one name for each side of it!

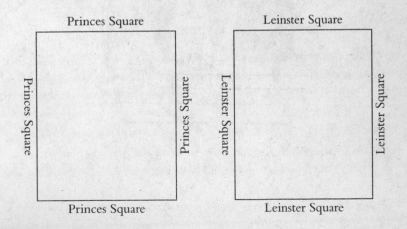

Chapter 22 Civil Servants★

English Civil Servants are very different from European Civil Servants.

In Europe (but not in Scandinavian countries), Civil Servants seem to think that they are soldiers. They shout and give you orders. When they speak, you hear the sound of guns. They cannot lose wars so they lose their papers instead. They think the most important thing in the world is to make more jobs for more Civil Servants.

In Europe, Civil Servants seem to think that they are soldiers.
They shout and give you orders.

★ A Civil Servant is a man or woman who works for the government.

A few Difficult People (who are not Civil Servants) make life hard for them. They ask too many questions or they have terrible problems.

European Civil Servants know what to do to these Difficult People. They make them wait in cold and dirty waiting rooms. They make them stand up all the time and they shout at them in a rude way. If a Difficult Person asks for something, the Civil Servant always smiles happily and says no.

Sometimes European Civil Servants play this clever little game: a Difficult Person goes to a Civil Servant's office on the third floor and asks a question.

'I don't know,' the Civil Servant says. 'Go and ask the Civil Servant in the office on the fifth floor.'

The Difficult Person goes to the office on the fifth floor and asks the question again. 'I don't know,' the Civil Servant on the fifth floor says. 'Go to the office on the second floor.'

The Difficult Person goes to the office on the second floor and asks the question again. 'Go to the third floor!' the Civil Servant on the second floor says.

So the Difficult Person goes back to the office on the third floor and speaks to the same Civil Servant in the same office again. 'But I told you to go to the fifth floor!' the first Civil Servant shouts.

The Difficult Person goes to the fifth floor and another Civil Servant sends him back to the second floor . . . Round and round and round.

European Civil Servants play this game all day until the Difficult Person is tired and goes home or goes mad and asks someone to take him to a hospital for mad people. If this happens, the Civil Servant says, 'Not here! Go to the office on the second floor . . .'

Soon the Difficult Person does not want to go to hospital and goes home.

But in England, Civil Servants are different. They do not think that they are soldiers, they think that they are businessmen. They are polite and kind and always smile and say yes when somebody asks a question. So everybody leaves British Civil Servants in their offices and they are able to spend all day quietly reading murder stories.

Why, you ask, do Difficult People in Britain leave British Civil Servants in their offices without asking them to do any work? I will tell you.

1 British Civil Servants write and speak a language that nobody understands.
2 Civil Servants never decide anything. They say that they will 'think about' something or 'think about it again'.
3 You can never find a British Civil Servant. Their job is to help people but if you try to find a Civil Servant, in fact he is never there. He is out on business, he is out for lunch, he is somewhere having tea or he is just out. Some Civil Servants are clever: they go for tea before they come back from lunch.

British Civil Servants are always polite. Before the war, British Civil Servants ordered an alien to leave the country. He asked to stay a few more weeks but they told him no, he had to leave. He stayed, and a short time later he got this letter:

> Dear Sir,
> We are very sorry to tell you that the Government has looked through all your papers again and has decided that you cannot stay in this country. We are terribly sorry to tell you that you must leave in the next twenty-four hours. If you do not, we will have to make you leave.
>
> Your servant,
> xxx

In Europe, rich and important people have friends, cousins and brothers that they know who are Civil Servants and who help them to get everything that they want. In England, if your friends and family are Civil Servants, they do nothing for you. This is the beautiful thing about England.

Chapter 23   British Newspapers

The Fact

There was some trouble on the Pacific Island of Charamak. A group of ten English and two American soldiers went to the island with Captain R.L.A.T.W. Tilbury. After a short fight against the Buburuk people they took 217 Buburuk prisoners, burned two large oil-refineries and put an end to the trouble. They then returned to their ship.

How do the British newspapers tell this story? Every newspaper tells it differently.

The Times
(one of Britain's greatest, most famous newspapers)

... It is important to understand that this fight was important but it was not very important. The Buburuk people were not easy to fight but, at the same time, they were not difficult to fight. We are not sure of the number of Buburuk prisoners but we think it is more than 216, but not more than 218.

In Parliament

A man from the government said:

> I can give this information about the Charamak oil-refineries. In the first half of the year the Army and most of – but not all – the Royal Air Force burned one-half more than three times the oil that the Army burned in the same months of last year. This is

seven and a half times more than the two-fifths that they burned two years ago and three-quarters more than twelve times one-sixth that they burned three years ago.

Someone jumped to his feet and asked if the Government knew that the British people were worried and angry because the Army went into Charamak but not into Ragamak.

The government speaker said, 'I have nothing to say about that, sir. I said everything when I spoke on 2nd August, 1892.'

Evening Standard
(a London evening newspaper)

The most interesting thing about the fight on Charamak is Reggie Tilbury. He is the fifth son of the Earl of Bayswater. He went to Oxford University and is good at several sports. When I talked to his wife (Lady Clarisse, the daughter of Lord Elasson) today, she wore a black suit and a small black and yellow hat. She said, 'Reggie was always very interested in war.' Later she said, 'It was very clever of him, wasn't it?'

Perhaps you decide to write a letter to *The Times* about all this:

Sir – About the fight on Charamak. The great English writer John Flat lived on Charamak in 1693. When he was there, he wrote his famous book, 'The Fish'.

Yours, etc.

The next day you will see this answer:

Sir, I am very pleased Mr . . . wrote about John Flat's book, 'The Fish'. I write to tell you that many people, like Mr . . ., think John Flat wrote 'The Fish' in 1693. He started the book in 1693, but he only finished it in 1694.

'Reggie was always very interested in war.'

If you write for an American newspaper, you just say this:

The Oklahoma Sun

'Americans win the war in the Pacific Ocean.'

Chapter 24   If Naturalized

The verb to naturalize shows that you must become British to be a natural person.

Look at the word 'natural' in a dictionary. It means 'real'. So if you are not naturalized, you are not a real person. To become a real person, you must become British. You must ask the British government to make you British. The government can say yes or it can say no.

If the government says yes and you become British, you must change the way that you think and live. You must not say the things that you think and you must look down on everything that you really are (an alien).

You must be like my English friend, Gregory Baker. He is an English lawyer. He looks down on these people: foreigners, Americans, Frenchmen, Irishmen, Scotsmen, Welshmen, Jews, workers, poor people, businessmen, writers, women, lawyers who are too rich, lawyers who are too poor. He does not like his mother because she is a good businesswoman; he does not like his wife because he does not like her family, and he does not like his brother because he is a soldier. Gregory does like his seven-year-old son because their noses are the same shape.

If you are naturalized, remember:

1 You must eat porridge for breakfast and say that you like it.
2 Speak English all the time, even with other 'aliens'. Do not speak the language of the country you came from. It is very un-English to understand or speak another language. If you must speak French, which is not too bad, then only speak it with a very bad accent.
3 Change your library at home. Only read books by English writers. Throw out famous Russian writers and buy books about English birds. Throw out famous French writers and read '*The Life of a Scottish Fish*' instead.
4 When you talk about the English, always say 'we'.

But be careful. I know a naturalized British man who repeated 'We Englishmen' when he was talking to another young man. The young man looked at him, took his pipe out of his mouth and said quietly, 'Sorry, sir, but I'm a Welshman.' Then he turned his back and walked away.

The same naturalized British man was listening to a conversation between two Englishwomen. 'The Japanese have shot down twenty-two aeroplanes in the last few days,' one of them said.

'What, ours?' the man asked the two women.

The Englishwoman looked at him coldly.

'No – *ours*,' she said.

ACTIVITIES

Preface–Chapter 8

Before you read

1   Look at the front cover of this book. What does this picture tell you about Englishmen? Can you still see people like this today? Are there people like this in your country?

2   Find these words in your dictionary.
    accent alien bell lawyer manners preface soul warning
    Now put the words in the right spaces.

    a ..... music   **e** health .....
    b door .....   **f** book's .....
    c criminal .....   **g** ..... spaceship
    d bad .....   **h** foreign .....

After you read

3   Choose the correct answer.

    a English people think you are clever if
        (i)   you talk about foreign writers.
        (ii) you're a doctor.
        (iii) you talk about the weather every day.

    b It's better
        (i)   to drink tea in hot weather than in cold weather.
        (ii) to have good manners than to have good food.
        (iii) to speak loudly than to speak quietly.

    c The English are usually
        (i)   polite to foreigners.
        (ii) friendly to foreigners.
        (iii) rude to foreigners.

4   Finish these sentences. An Englishman will

    a smile and wait if you ...
    b not forgive you if you ...
    c think you are clever, polite and amusing if you ...
    d say he quite likes you if he ...
    e think you are very foreign and strange if you ...
    f think you probably speak good English if you ...

5 What does George Mikes find strange about
  a hot water bottles?   **b** cats?   **c** radio weather reports?

Chapters 9–18
Before you read

6 Think of *three* ways to be rude in your country. Are these things also rude in England, do you think?

7 Find these words in your dictionary.
  compromise   hypocrite   pleasure   queue   sphinx
  Which of these words is
  a something made of stone?
  b something you enjoy?
  c something you do at a bus-stop?
  d something you do to end a disagreement?
  e someone who says one thing and does another?

After you read

8 Some of these sentences are not true. Which ones, and why?
  a English people think clever people are dishonest.
  b Pubs are open at 4 o'clock in the afternoon.
  c The English don't like fires in their houses.
  d The English like singing when nobody can hear them.
  e English families practise queueing at home.
  f Intellectuals like big beards.

9 Which of these things do the English like?
  good books / good hotels / good food / good clothes
  intelligent conversation / playing with toys / golf

Chapters 19–24
Before you read

10 Find these words in your dictionary.
  bend   mad   naturalized   park   porridge   refinery
  Now put the words in the right spaces.
  a a sharp .....   **c** go .....   **e** ..... dangerously
  b cold .....   **d** oil .....   **f** ..... Englishman

11 Imagine that you can change the driving rules in your country. What rules will you change, and why?

After you read

12 How do the English
   a make roads safe?
   b enjoy an afternoon's holiday?
   c make sure nobody can find their house?
   d How do bus drivers make passengers angry?
   e How do civil servants succeed in having an easy life?

13 Work in pairs. Act out this conversation between a civil servant and someone who wants to be naturalized.

   Student A: You want to be naturalized. Tell the civil servant why you like the English, and why you want to live here for the rest of your life.

   Student B: You are a civil servant. Ask a lot of difficult questions, then politely explain to the person why his or her request is not possible.

Writing

14 'This book tells foreigners everything they need to know about the English.' Do you agree? Or are there other strange things about the English that are not in this book? Write about it for a student magazine.

15 Write a letter to an English friend who is visiting your country for the first time. Describe some of the strange things that he or she will find in your country.

16 What is the funniest or strangest thing that has happened to you in another country? Write a story about it. Describe your feelings at the time.

17 You work for the government of your country. Write a report saying what things about the English way of life are a good idea for your country. Say why.

Answers for the Activities in this book are published in our free resource packs for teachers, the Penguin Readers Factsheets, or available on a separate sheet. Please write to your local Pearson Education office or to: Marketing Department, Penguin Longman Publishing, 5 Bentinck Street, London W1M 5RN.